Vegetables
Las Verduras

Words in English and Spanish

Morgan Kadric

All titles, text, logos, and illustrations Copyright © 2023 by Alderwood Publishing LLC.
All rights reserved, including the right of complete or partial reproduction in any form.
Published by Alderwood Publishing LLC.
Written, illustrated, and designed by Morgan Kadric. Translated into Spanish by Morgan Kadric, Carla Wood, and Daniel Villalobos-Terrazas.
No part of this book may be used or reproduced in any manner without written permission from Alderwood Publishing LLC.
www.alderwoodpublishing.com
KDP ISBN 9798372172340

Todos los títulos, textos, logotipos e ilustraciones son propiedad intelectual © 2023 de Alderwood Publishing LLC.
Todos los derechos reservados, incluido el derecho de reproducción total o parcial en cualquier forma.
Publicado por Alderwood Publishing LLC.
Escrito, ilustrado y diseñado por Morgan Kadric. Traducido al español por Morgan Kadric, Carla Wood, y Daniel Villalobos-Terrazas.
Ninguna parte de este libro se puede usar o reproducir de ninguna manera sin el permiso por escrito de Alderwood Publishing LLC.
www.alderwoodpublishing.com
KDP ISBN 9798372172340

Disclosure: Alderwood Publishing LLC attempted to provide the most accurate translation of the original material in English, but due to the nuances of translation to a foreign language and various geographical linguistic differences, variations and inconsistencies may exist. Any discrepancies or differences created from the translation are not binding and have no legal effect for compliance or enforcement purposes. Alderwood Publishing LLC is not liable for any losses caused by reliance on translations.

Divulgación: Alderwood Publishing LLC intentó proporcionar la traducción más precisa del material original en inglés, pero debido a los matices de la traducción a un idioma extranjero y varias diferencias lingüísticas geográficas, pueden existir variaciones e inconsistencias. Cualquier discrepancia o diferencia creada a partir de la traducción no es vinculante y no tiene ningún efecto legal a efectos de cumplimiento o aplicación. Alderwood Publishing LLC no es responsable de ninguna pérdida causada por confiar en las traducciones.

*For Sedin & Ajdin-
You are my everything.*

Spanish Alphabet (El Alfabeto)

Letter	Letter Name	Pronunciation
a	a	ah
b	be	beh
c	ce	seh
ch	che	cheh
d	de	deh
e	e	eh
f	efe	eff-eh
g	ge	heh
h	hache	ach-eh
i	i	ee
j	jota	ho-ta
k	ka	ka
l	ele	el-leh
ll	elle	eh-yeh
m	eme	eh-meh
n	ene	eh-neh
ñ	eñe	en-yeh
o	o	oh
p	pe	peh
q	cu	koo
r	ere	ar-eh
rr	erre	er-reh
s	ese	es-seh
t	te	teh
u	u	oo
v	ve	veh
w	doble ve	doh-bleh veh
x	equis	eh-kees
y	i griega	e-grie-ga
z	zeta	ze-tah

Carrot

Zanahoria

Cabbage

Repollo

Mushrooms

Champiñones

Green Beans

Judías Verdes

Radishes

Rábanos

Peas

Chícharos

Garlic

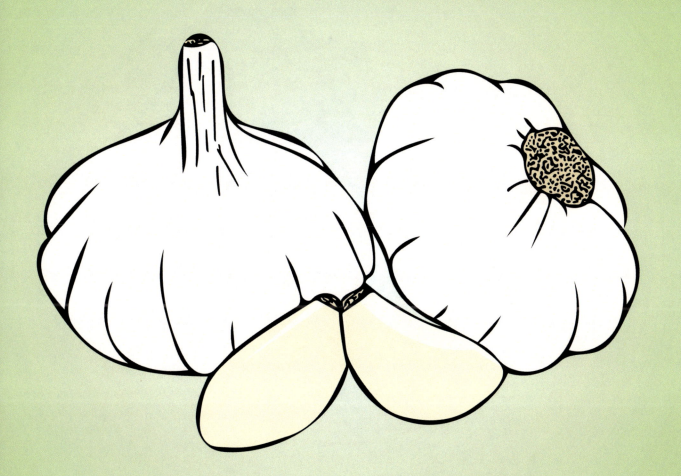

Ajo

Celery

Apio

Tomato

Tomate

Eggplant

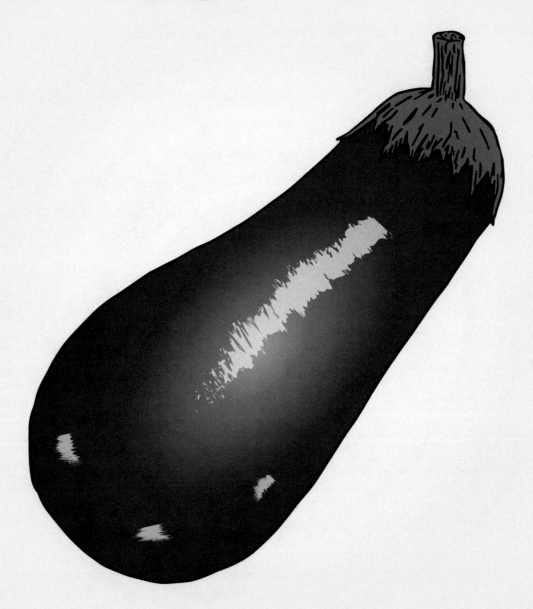

Berenjena

Pumpkin

Calabaza

Cucumber

Pepino

Pepper

Pimiento

Lettuce

Lechuga

Onion

Cebolla

Broccoli

Brócoli

Sweet Potato

Camote

Asparagus

Espárrago

Beans

Frijoles

Corn

Elote

Leek

Puerro

Zucchini

Calabacita

Potato

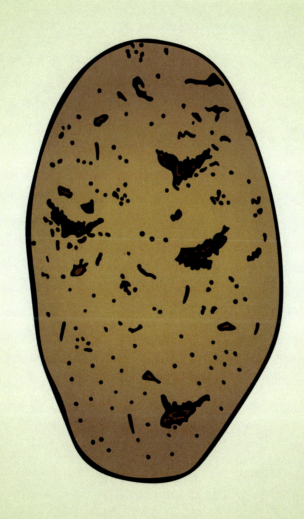

Papa

Spinach

Espinaca

Avocado

Aguacate

TEACH ME!
SPANISH
LANGUAGE BASICS

Check out other books in the series at
alderwoodpublishing.com

Made in the USA
Middletown, DE
25 September 2023

39294865R10018